Gifts of Love

Gifts of Love

A selection of unusual love poetry

Illustrated and Edited by Ferris Cook

Stewart, Tabori & Chang
New York

Illustrations and compilation copyright © 2000 by Ferris Cook

Project Editor: H. D. R. Campbell

Designer: Stephanie Whitehouse

A list of acknowledgments to copyright owners can be found at the back of this volume on pages 78 and 79.

Published in 2000 by

Stewart, Tabori & Chang
A division of U.S. Media Holdings, Inc.
115 West 18th Street
New York, NY 10011

Distributed in Canada by
General Publishing Company Ltd.
30 Lesmill Road
Don Mills, Ontario, Canada M3B 2T6

Library of Congress Cataloging-in-Publication Data
Gifts of love: a selection of love poetry / edited and illustrated by Ferris Cook.
    p. cm.
   ISBN 1-55670-983-8 (hc.)
    I. Love poetry. I. Cook, Ferris.
PN6110.L6G54 2000
808.81'93543—dc21   99-046421

The text of this book was composed in Paliard.

Printed in Hong Kong

10 9 8 7 6 5 4 3 2 1

First Printing

For Mer

Contents

from One Word More

I shall never, in the years remaining,
Paint you pictures, no, nor carve you statues,
Make you music that should all-express me;
So it seems: I stand on my attainment.
This of verse alone, one life allows me;
Verse and nothing else have I to give you.
Other heights in other lives, God willing:
All the gifts from all the heights, your own, Love!

ROBERT BROWNING
(1812–1889)

The April Lovers

Green is happening.
Through the sweet expectant chill
Of a northern spring
We have gone without will,

Without fear, without reason,
Trusting to the power
Of a fickle season,
Of a passionate hour,

To mature, to sustain
Till the plan uncovers
In the sun and rain.
Early lovers

 Never question much
What is quietly beating
Through the music and the touch
And the mouths meeting.

VIRGINIA ADAIR
(b. 1913)

The Telephone

"When I was just as far as I could walk
From here today,
There was an hour

All still
When leaning with my head against a flower
I heard you talk.
Don't say I didn't, for I heard you say—
You spoke from that flower on the windowsill—
Do you remember what it was you said?"

"First tell me what it was you thought you heard."

"Having found the flower and driven a bee away,
I leaned my head,
And holding by the stalk,
I listened and I thought I caught the word—
What was it? Did you call me by my name?
Or did you say—
Someone said 'Come'—I heard it as I bowed."

"I may have thought as much, but not aloud."

"Well, so I came."

ROBERT FROST
(1874–1963)

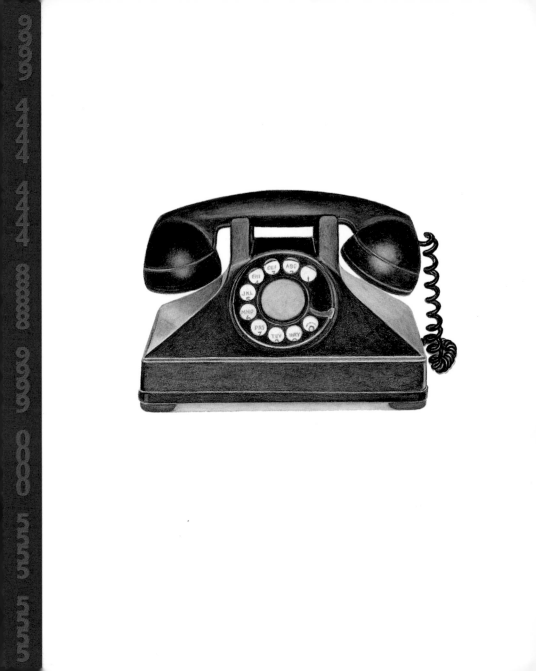

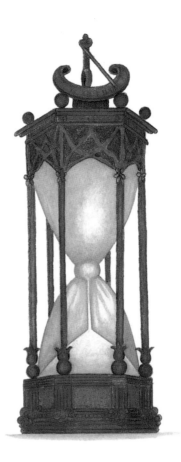

Silent Noon

Your hands lie open in the long fresh grass,—
The finger-points look through like rosy blooms:
Your eyes smile peace. The pasture gleams and glooms
'Neath billowing skies that scatter and amass.
All round our nest, far as the eye can pass,
Are golden kingcup-fields with silver edge
Where the cow-parsley skirts the hawthorn-hedge.
'Tis visible silence, still as the hour-glass.
Deep in the sun-searched growths the dragon-fly
Hangs like a blue thread loosened from the sky:—
So this wing'd hour is dropped to us from above.
Oh! clasp we to our hearts, for deathless dower,
This close-companioned inarticulate hour
When twofold silence was the song of love.

DANTE GABRIEL ROSSETTI
(1828—1882)

March 4th

Improve your finances.

The high ones, Berryman said, die, die, die.
You look up and who is there?
Daddy's not there shaking his money cane.
Mother's not there waving dollars good-bye
or coughing diamonds into her hanky. Not a forbear,
not an aunt or a chick to call me by name,
not the gardener with his candy dimes and tickles,
not grandpa with his bag full of nickels.

They are all embalmed with their cash
and there is no one here but us kids.
You and me lapping stamps and paying
the bills, shoveling up the beans and the hash.
Our checks are pale. Our wallets are invalids.
Past due, past due, is what our bills are saying
and yet we kiss in every corner, scuffing the dust
and the cat. Love rises like bread as we go bust.

ANNE SEXTON
(1928–1974)

16

Argument to Love as a Person

The cut rhododendron branches
flowered in our sunless flat.
Don't complain to me, dear,
that I waste your life in poverty:
you and the cuttings prove: Those
that have it in them to be beautiful
flower wherever they are!, although
they are, like everything else, ephemeral.
Freedom is as mortal as tyranny.

ALAN DUGAN
(b. 1923)

A Señorita's Bouquet

I thought of the flowers I picked for her
coming home from the movies one night,
a metaphor in the eyes of the cat
in our alley.

Later I came across her dried corsage
from the wedding.
My heart so full of love
I crumbled the flowers,
a yellow dust like Bull Durham
clung to my fingers,
more softness to it
than her wedding flowers.

GILBERT SORRENTINO
(b. 1929)

Your Feet

When I can not look at your face
I look at your feet.

Your feet of arched bone,
your hard little feet.

I know that they support you,
and that your gentle weight
rises upon them.

Your waist and your breasts,
the doubled purple
of your nipples,
the sockets of your eyes
that have just flown away,
your wide fruit mouth,
your red tresses,
my little tower.

But I love your feet
only because they walked
upon the earth and upon
the wind and upon the waters,
until they found me.

PABLO NERUDA
(1904–1973)

I Wish I Could Remember

Era già l'ora che volge il desio.—DANTE.
Ricorro al tempo ch'io vi vidi prima.—PETRARCA.

I wish I could remember that first day,
    First hour, first moment of your meeting me,
    If bright or dim the season, it might be
Summer or Winter for aught I can say;
So unrecorded did it slip away,
    So blind was I to see and to foresee,
    So dull to mark the budding of my tree
That would not blossom yet for many a May.
If only I could recollect it, such
    A day of days! I let it come and go
    As traceless as a thaw of bygone snow;
It seemed to mean so little, meant so much;
If only now I could recall that touch,
    First touch of hand in hand—Did one but know!

CHRISTINA ROSSETTI
(1830–1894)

The Good-Morrow

I wonder, by my troth, what thou and I
Did, till we loved? were we not weaned till then?
But sucked on country pleasures, childishly?
Or snored we in the Seven Sleepers' den?
'Twas so; but this, all pleasures fancies be;
If ever any beauty I did see,
Which I desired, and got, 'twas but a dream of thee.

And now good-morrow to our waking souls,
Which watch not one another out of fear;
For love all love of other sights controls,
And makes one little room an everywhere.
Let sea-discoverers to new worlds have gone;
Let maps to other, worlds on worlds have shown,
Let us possess one world; each hath one, and is one.

My face in thine eye, thine in mine appears,
And true plain hearts do in the faces rest;
Where can we find two fitter hemispheres
Without sharp north, without declining west?
Whatever dies, was not mixed equally;
If our two loves be one, or thou and I
Love just alike in all, none of these loves can die.

JOHN DONNE
(1573–1631)

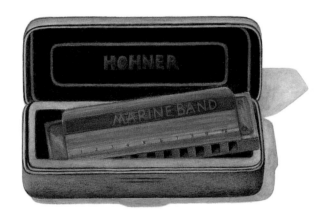

Love Song for Antonia

If I should sing
All of my songs for you
And you would not listen to them,
If I should build
All of my dream houses for you
And you would never live in them,
If I should give
All of my hopes to you
And you would laugh and say: I do not care,
Still I would give you my love
Which is more than my songs,
More than any houses of dreams,
Or dreams of houses—
I would still give you my love
Though you never looked at me.

LANGSTON HUGHES
(1902—1967)

Sonnet XXV

Why are thou silent? Is thy love a plant
Of such weak fibre that the treacherous air
Of absence withers what was once so fair?
Is there no debt to pay, no boon to grant?
Yet have my thoughts for thee been vigilant—
Bound to thy service with unceasing care,
The mind's least generous wish a mendicant
For nought but what thy happiness could spare.
Speak!—though this soft warm heart, once free to hold
A thousand tender pleasures, thine and mine,
Be left more desolate, more dreary cold
Than a forsaken bird's-nest filled with snow
'Mid its own bush of leafless eglantine—
Speak, that my torturing doubts their end may know!

WILLIAM WORDSWORTH
(1770–1850)

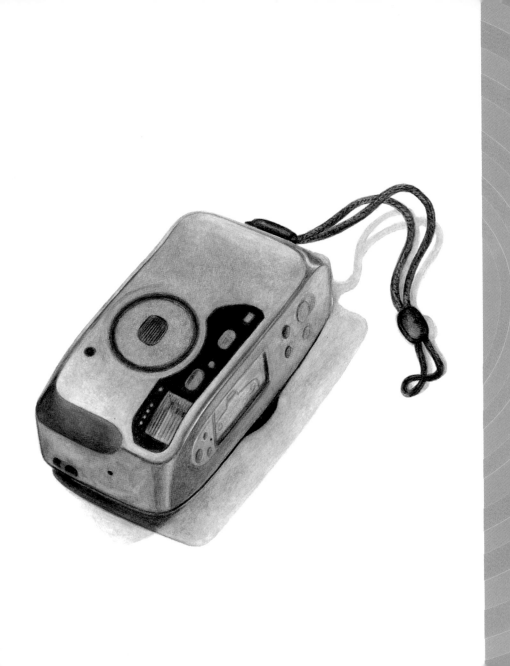

A Deep-sworn Vow

Others because you did not keep
That deep-sworn vow have been friends of mine;
Yet always when I look death in the face,
When I clamber to the heights of sleep,
Or when I grow excited with wine,
Suddenly I meet your face.

WILLIAM BUTLER YEATS
(1865 – 1939)

Answer to a Child's Question

Do you ask what the birds say? The Sparrow, the Dove,
The Linnet and Thrush say, "I love and I love!"
In the winter they're silent—the wind is so strong;
What it says, I don't know, but it sings a loud song.
But green leaves, and blossoms, and sunny warm weather,
And singing, and loving—all come back together.
But the Lark is so brimful of gladness and love,
The green fields below him, the blue sky above,
That he sings, and he sings, and for ever sings he—
"I love my Love, and my Love loves me!"

SAMUEL TAYLOR COLERIDGE
(1772–1834)

Nurse's Song

When the voices of children are heard on the green
    And laughing is heard on the hill,
My heart is at rest within my breast,
    And everything else is still.

"Then come home, my children, the sun is gone down,
    And the dews of the night arise;
Come, come, leave off play, and let us away
    Till the morning appears in the skies."

"No, no, let us play, for it is yet day,
    And we cannot go to sleep;
Besides in the sky the little birds fly,
    And the hills are all covered with sheep."

"Well, well, go and play till the light fades away,
    And then go home to bed."
The little ones leaped and shouted and laughed;
    And all the hills echoèd.

WILLIAM BLAKE
(1757–1827)

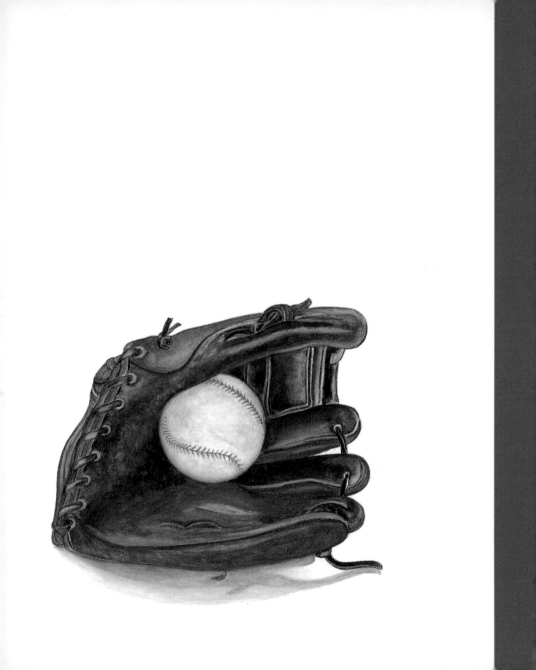

Baseball

The ball once struck off,
Away flies the boy
To the next destined post
And then home with joy.

ANONYMOUS

Romance

I will make you brooches and toys for your delight
Of bird-song at morning and star-shine at night.
I will make a palace fit for you and me,
Of green days in forests and blue days at sea.

I will make my kitchen, and you shall keep your room,
Where white flows the river and bright blows the broom,
And you shall wash your linen and keep your body white
In rainfall at morning and dewfall at night.

And this shall be for music when no one else is near,
The fine song for singing, the rare song to hear!
That only I remember, that only you admire,
Of the broad road that stretches and the roadside fire.

ROBERT LOUIS STEVENSON
(1850–1894)

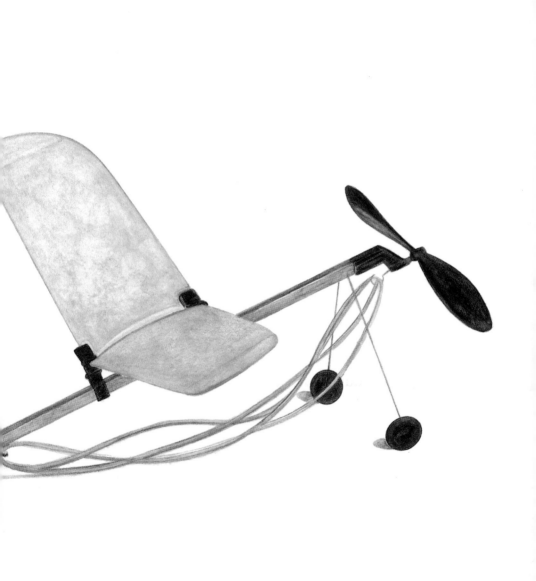

In Love, If Love Be Love

In Love, if Love be Love, if Love be ours,
Faith and unfaith can ne'er be equal powers:
Unfaith in aught is want of faith in all.

It is the little rift within the lute
That by and by will make the music mute,
And ever widening slowly silence all.

The little rift within the lover's lute
Or little pitted speck in garnered fruit,
That rotting inward slowly moulders all.

It is not worth the keeping: let it go:
But shall it? answer, darling, answer, no.
And trust me not at all or all in all.

ALFRED TENNYSON
(1809–1892)

40

Sonnet XIV

If thou must love me, let it be for naught
Except for love's sake only. Do not say,
"I love her for her smile—her look—her way
Of speaking gently—for a trick of thought
That falls in well with mine, and certes brought
A sense of pleasant ease on such a day"—
For these things in themselves, Belovèd, may
Be changed, or change for thee—and love, so wrought,
May be unwrought so. Neither love me for
Thine own dear pity's wiping my cheeks dry:
A creature might forget to weep, who bore
Thy comfort long, and lose thy love thereby!
But love me for love's sake, that evermore
Thou may'st love on, through love's eternity.

ELIZABETH BARRETT BROWNING
(1806—1861)

The Flaming Rose

Lovers, the stuff you're woven of is spring,
is wind and water, earth and sun.
You've hills in your heaving chests,
blossoming fields in your eyes:
    go forth with the spring you share
and freely drink of the sweet milk
the wanton panther offers you today—
soon enough she'll stalk you foully in your path.

Walk on when the tilt of the globe
points toward the summer solstice,
with the almond fully leaved, the violet withered,
    thirst close at hand, springs to slake it near—
on toward the fullness of love's afternoon,
holding in your hands the flaming rose.

ANTONIO MACHADO
(1875–1939)

Two Lovers

Two lovers by a moss-grown spring:
    They leaned soft cheeks together there,
    Mingled the dark and sunny hair,
And heard the wooing thrushes sing.
        O budding time!
        O love's blest prime!

Two wedded from the portal stept:
    The bells made happy carolings,
    The air was soft as fanning wings,
White petals on the pathway slept.
        O pure-eyed bride!
        O tender pride!

Two faces o'er a cradle bent:
    Two hands above the head were locked:
    These pressed each other while they rocked,
Those watched a life that love had sent.
        O solemn hour!
        O hidden power!

Two parents by the evening fire:
   The red light fell about their knees
   On heads that rose by slow degrees
Like buds upon the lily spire.
        O patient life!
        O tender strife!

The two still sat together there,
   The red light shone about their knees;
   But all the heads by slow degrees
Had gone and left that lonely pair.
        O voyage fast!
        O vanished past!

The red light shone upon the floor
   And made the space between them wide;
   They drew their chairs up side by side,
Their pale cheeks joined, and said, "Once more!"
        O memories!
        O past that is!

GEORGE ELIOT
(1819–1880)

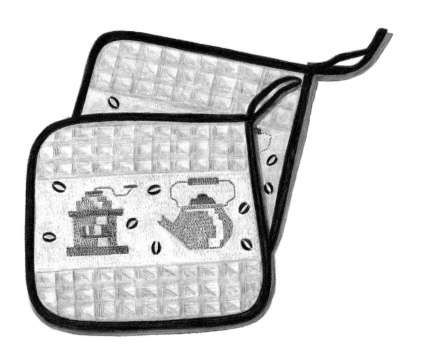

Love Song

Sweep the house clean,
hang fresh curtains
in the windows
put on a new dress
and come with me!
The elm is scattering
its little loaves
of sweet smells
from a white sky!
Who shall hear of us
in the time to come?
Let him say there was
a burst of fragrance
from black branches.

WILLIAM CARLOS WILLIAMS
(1883–1963)

A Valentine

Oh! little loveliest lady mine,
What shall I send for your valentine?
Summer and flowers are far away;
Gloomy old Winter is king to-day;
Buds will not blow, and sun will not shine:
What shall I do for a valentine?

I've searched the gardens all through and through
For a bud to tell of my love so true;
But buds are asleep, and blossoms are dead,
And the snow beats down on my poor little head:
So, little loveliest lady mine,
Here is my heart for your valentine!

LAURA ELIZABETH RICHARDS
(1850−1943)

On an Anniversary

Thirty years and more go by
In the blinking of an eye,
    And you are still the same
As when first you took my name.

Much the same blush now as then
Glimmers through the peach-pale skin.
    Time (but as with a glove)
Lightly touches you, my love.

Stand with me a minute still
While night climbs our little hill.
    Below, the lights of cars
Move, and overhead the stars.

The estranging years that come,
Come and go, and we are home.
    Time joins us as a friend,
And the evening has no end.

DONALD JUSTICE
(b.1925)

One Perfect Rose

A single flow'r he sent me, since we met.
    All tenderly his messenger he chose;
Deep-hearted, pure, with scented dew still wet
    One perfect rose.

I knew the language of the floweret;
    'My fragile leaves,' it said, 'his heart enclose.'
Love long has taken for his amulet
    One perfect rose.

Why is it no one ever sent me yet
    One perfect limousine, do you suppose?
Ah no, it's always just my luck to get
    One perfect rose.

DOROTHY PARKER
(1893–1967)

For an Amorous Lady

'Most mammals like caresses, in the sense in which we
usually take the word, whereas other creatures, even
tame snakes, prefer giving to receiving them.'
FROM A NATURAL-HISTORY BOOK

The pensive gnu, the staid aardvark,
Accept caresses in the dark;
The bear, equipped with paw and snout,
Would rather take than dish it out.
But snakes, both poisonous and garter,
In love are never known to barter;
The worm, though dank, is sensitive:
His noble nature bids him *give*.

But you, my dearest, have a soul
Encompassing fish, flesh, and fowl.
When amorous arts we would pursue,
You can, with pleasure, bill *or* coo.
You are, in truth, one in a million,
At once mammalian and reptilian.

THEODORE ROETHKE
(1908 – 1963)

To F—

Beloved! amid the earnest woes
    That crowd around my earthly path—
(Drear path, alas! where grows
Not even one lonely rose—
    My soul at least a solace hath
In dreams of thee, and therein knows
An Eden of bland repose.

And thus thy memory is to me
    Like some enchanted far-off isle
In some tumultuous sea—
Some ocean throbbing far and free
    With storms—but where meanwhile
Serenest skies continually
    Just o'er that one bright island smile.

EDGAR ALLAN POE
(1809—1849)

Longing

Come to me in my dreams, and then
By day I shall be well again!
For then the night will more than pay
The hopeless longing of the day.

Come, as thou cam'st a thousand times,
A messenger from radiant climes,
And smile on thy new world, and be
As kind to others as to me!

Or, as thou never cam'st in sooth,
Come now, and let me dream it truth;
And part my hair, and kiss my brow,
And say: *My love! why sufferest thou?*

Come to me in my dreams, and then
By day I shall be well again!
For then the night will more than pay
The hopeless longing of the day.

MATTHEW ARNOLD
(1822 – 1888)

A Decade

When you came, you were like red wine and honey,
And the taste of you burnt my mouth with its sweetness.
Now you are like morning bread,
Smooth and pleasant.
I hardly taste you at all for I know your savour,
But I am completely nourished.

AMY LOWELL
(1874 – 1925)

Natural Music

The old voice of the ocean, the bird-chatter
   of little rivers,
(Winter has given them gold for silver
To stain their water and bladed green for brown
   to line their banks)
From different throats intone one language.
So I believe if we were strong enough to listen without
Divisions of desire and terror
To the storm of the sick nations, the rage of
   the hunger-smitten cities,
Those voices also would be found
Clean as a child's; or like some girls' breathing
   who dances alone
By the ocean-shore, dreaming of lovers.

ROBINSON JEFFERS
(1887–1962)

Good and Bad Weather

It does not bother me if outside
winter spreads fog, clouds, and cold.
Spring is within me, true joy.
Laughter is a sun ray, all pure gold,
there is no other garden like love,
the warmth of song melts all the snows.

What good is it that outside spring
sends up flowers and sows greenness!
I have winter within me when the heart hurts.
The sigh blots out the most brilliant sun;
if you have sorrow May resembles December,
tears are colder than the cold snow.

C. P. CAVAFY
(1863–1933)

The More Loving One

Looking up at the stars, I know quite well
That, for all they care, I can go to hell,
But on earth indifference is the least
We have to dread from man or beast.

How should we like it were stars to burn
With a passion for us we could not return?
If equal affection cannot be,
Let the more loving one be me.

Admirer as I think I am
Of stars that do not give a damn,
I cannot, now I see them, say
I missed one terribly all day.

Were all stars to disappear or die,
I should learn to look at an empty sky
And feel its total dark sublime,
Though this might take me a little time.

W. H. AUDEN
(1907–1973)

For Ring-Givers

Given the gift of a ring,
what circle does it close?
What does it say, passing
from lover to lover?
That love, encircled so,
rings for ever?

Or is it the round of love?
Does the ring say
"So must love move,
and in its altering weather,
you two will turn away
as now you turn together"?

Is the ring given or lent?
Does love ring round us
or do we ring round it?
Ring-giver, be warned.
Are you, in turn, expecting
love or the ring returned?

ALASTAIR REID
(b.1926)

This Thing You Give Me

This thing you give me, is it love you feel,
Or love you feign? You give it: that suffices me.
Though in years no novice,
Let me be one in delusion.
The gods give us little, and that little is false.
Yet, if they give it, for all its falseness
The gift is real. I take it
And close my eyes: 'tis enough.
Why ask for more?

FERNANDO PESSOA
(Ricardo Reis)
(1888 – 1935)

Birthday Bush

Our bush bloomed, soon dropped
its fuchsia chalices. Rags
on the ground that were luscious
cups and trumpets, promises and brags.

A sprinkle of dark dots showed entry
into each silk cone. Down among
crisp pistils thirsty bumblebees
probed. Buds flared in a bunch

from tender stems. Sudden
vivid big bouquets
appeared just before our birthdays!
A galaxy our burning bush,

blissful explosion. Brief
effusion. Brief as these
words. I sweep away a trash
of crimson petals.

MAY SWENSON
(1919−1989)

I Loved You

I loved you; and perhaps in love's dead embers,
Not quite extinguished, some few sparks remain.
Let it not fret you if your heart remembers:
I would not cause you grief or give you pain.
I loved you hopelessly, confession fleeing,
Now far too jealous, now too shy to tell.
With all my heart I loved you, all my being—
God grant another love you half so well!

ALEXANDER PUSHKIN
(1799–1837)

Sometimes with One I Love

Sometimes with one I love I fill myself with rage for fear
    I effuse unreturn'd love,
But now I think there is no unreturn'd love, the pay is certain
    one way or another.
(I loved a certain person ardently, and my love was not
    return'd,
Yet out of that I have written these songs.)

WALT WHITMAN
(1819−1892)

A Slice of Wedding Cake

Why have such scores of lovely, gifted girls
    Married impossible men?
Simple self-sacrifice may be ruled out,
    And missionary endeavour, nine times out of ten.

Repeat 'impossible men': not merely rustic,
    Foul-tempered or depraved
(Dramatic foils chosen to show the world
    How well women behave, and always have behaved).

Impossible men: idle, illiterate,
    Self-pitying, dirty, sly,
For whose appearance even in City parks
    Excuses must be made to casual passers-by.

Has God's supply of tolerable husbands
    Fallen, in fact, so low?
Or do I always over-value woman
    At the expense of man?
            Do I?
                It might be so.

ROBERT GRAVES
(1895 – 1985)

Hyacinth

I am in love with him to whom a hyacinth is dearer
Than I shall ever be dear.
On nights when the field-mice are abroad he cannot sleep:
He hears their narrow teeth at the bulbs of his hyacinths.
But the gnawing at my heart he does not hear.

EDNA ST. VINCENT MILLAY
(1892–1950)

Parting Gift

I cannot give you the Metropolitan Tower;
I cannot give you heaven;
Nor the nine Visigoth crowns in the Cluny Museum;
Nor happiness, even.
But I can give you a very small purse
Made out of field-mouse skin,
With a painted picture of the universe
And seven blue tears therein.

I cannot give you the island of Capri;
I cannot give you beauty;
Nor bake you marvellous crusty cherry pies
With love and duty.
But I can give you a very little locket
Made out of wildcat hide:
Put it into your left-hand pocket
And never look inside.

ELINOR WYLIE
(1885—1928)

Acknowledgments

Thanks are due to the following copyright holders for permission to reprint poems in this volume:

Virginia Adair: "The April Lovers" from ANTS ON THE MELON by Virginia Hamilton Adair. Copyright © 1996 by Virginia Hamilton Adair. Reprinted by permission of Random House, Inc.

W. H. Auden: "The More Loving One" from COLLECTED SHORTER POEMS: 1927–1957 by W. H. Auden. Copyright © 1966 Faber & Faber Ltd. Copyright © 1958 by W. H. Auden. Renewed. Used by permission of Curtis Brown Ltd. and Faber & Faber Ltd.

C. P. Cavafy: "Good and Bad Weather" from THE COMPLETE POEMS OF CAVAFY by C. P. Cavafy. Copyright © 1961 and renewed © 1989 by Rae Dalven. Reprinted by permission of Harcourt, Inc. and The Hogarth Press.

Alan Dugan: "Argument to Love as a Person" from NEW AND COLLECTED POEMS 1961–1983 by Alan Dugan. Copyright © 1961, 1962, 1968, 1972, 1973, 1974, 1983 by Alan Dugan. Reprinted by permission of The Ecco Press.

Robert Frost: "The Telephone" from THE POETRY OF ROBERT FROST, edited by Edward Connery Lathem. Copyright © 1916, 1944 by Robert Frost. Copyright 1969 by Henry Holt and Company. Reprinted by permission of Henry Holt and Company, LLC.

Robert Graves: "A Slice of Wedding Cake" from THE COMPLETE POEMS by Robert Graves, edited by Beryl Graves and Dunstan Ward. Copyright © 1997. Reprinted by permission of Carcanet Press Limited.

Langston Hughes: "Love Song for Antonia" from COLLECTED POEMS by Langston Hughes. Copyright © 1994 by The Estate of Langston Hughes. Reprinted by permission of Alfred A. Knopf, Inc. and Harold Ober Associates Inc.

Robinson Jeffers: "Natural Music" from THE COLLECTED POETRY OF ROBINSON JEFFERS, THREE VOLUMES by Robinson Jeffers, edited by Tim Hunt. Copyright © 1938, renewed 1966 by Donnan Jeffers and Garth Jeffers. Copyright transferred 1995 to the Board of Trustees of the Leland Stanford Junior University. Used by permission of the publishers, Stanford University Press.

Donald Justice: "On an Anniversary" from NEW AND SELECTED POEMS by Donald Justice. Copyright © 1995 by Donald Justice. Reprinted by permission of Alfred A. Knopf, Inc.

Antonio Machado: "The Flaming Rose" from ANTONIO MACHADO: SELECTED POEMS by Antonio Machado, ed. Alan S. Trueblood, Cambridge, Mass.: Harvard University Press. Copyright © 1982 by the President and Fellows of Harvard College. Reprinted by permission of the publisher.

Edna St. Vincent Millay: "Hyacinth" from COLLECTED POEMS by Edna St. Vincent Millay, HarperCollins. Copyright © 1923, 1951 by Edna St. Vincent Millay and Norma Millay Ellis. All rights reserved. Reprinted by permission of Elizabeth Barnett, literary executor.

Pablo Neruda: "Your Feet" from THE CAPTAIN'S VERSES by Pablo Neruda. Translated by Donald D. Walsh. Copyright © 1972 by Pablo Neruda and Donald D. Walsh. Reprinted by permission of New Directions Publishing Corp.

Dorothy Parker: "One Perfect Rose" from THE PORTABLE DOROTHY PARKER by Dorothy Parker. Copyright 1926, renewed © 1954 by Dorothy Parker. Used by permission of Viking Penguin, a division of Penguin Putnam Inc. and by permission of Gerald Duckworth & Co. Ltd.